Keto Bread Cookbook

50 Low-Carb, Keto-Friendly Breads for Every Meal

Elena Baker

Chapter 1: Breakfast Recipes

Breakfast Muffins

Serves: 4 muffins **Nutritional Values:** Calories: 373.8, Total Fat: 31.7 g, Saturated Fat: 4.8 g, Carbs: 9.1 g,

Sugars: 2 g,

Protein: 16.6 g

Ingredients:

- For the flavorings:
- 4 oz Bacon, chopped
- ½ cup Scallions, chopped

Dry ingredients:

- 1¼ cups Almond Flour
- ¼ tsp Baking Soda
- ½ tsp Salt
- 1 tsp Baking Powder

Wet ingredients:

- ½ cup Coconut Milk
- 2 Tbsp Olive Oil
- 1 Egg
- ½ tsp White Vinegar

For the muffins:

- 4 Eggs

Directions:

1. Preheat your oven to 350F / 175C. Grease your muffin tin or cups and set aside.
2. Heat a skillet on high, add the bacon and fry until browned. Transfer to a paper towel and leave to drain, chop and set aside.
3. Combine the dry ingredients and set aside.
4. Mix together the wet ingredients and add them to the dry mix. Stir just to combine, do not overmix.
5. Add the chopped fried bacon along with the scallions, mix to incorporate and set aside.
6. Scoop 3 tablespoons of batter into each of 4 muffin cups, flatten and make a small dent into the middle of the batter. Crack the eggs and gently set an egg into each of the batter dents. Fill the cups with the remaining batter and bake in the preheated oven for about 20 minutes.
7. Once golden brown, remove from the oven and leave to rest for about 5-10 minutes before serving.

Colorful Breakfast Muffins

Serves: 6 muffins

Nutritional Values:

Calories: 73.4, Total Fat: 4.1 g, Saturated Fat: 1.3 g, Carbs: 3.4 g, Sugars: 0.6 g, Protein: 5.9 g

Ingredients:

- 3 Spring Onions, chopped
- 1 Bell Pepper, diced
- 4 Cherry Tomatoes, chopped
- 1 handful Spinach
- 1/4 - 1/2 tsp Salt
- 6 Eggs
- 1 tsp Curry Powder

Directions:

1. Preheat your oven to 390F / 200C. Grease your muffin tin and set aside.
2. Add the vegetables to a bowl, season with salt and toss. Beat the eggs and add them to the veggies and mix well. Sprinkle with the curry powder.
3. Pour the batter into the prepared muffin tin and bake in the preheated oven for about 15- 20 minutes.
4. Once baked, remove from the oven, allow to cool before serving.

Goat Cheese Crackers

Prep time: 5 minutes

- Cooking time: 15 minutes
- Servings: 12

Nutritional Values:

- Calories 99
- Total carbs 2 g
- Protein 4 g
- Total fat 8 g

Ingredients:

- 6 oz goat cheese
- ½ cup coconut flour
- 4 tbsp butter
- 2 tbsp fresh rosemary
- 1 tsp baking powder

Directions:

1. In a food processor combine all ingredients and process until smooth.
2. Roll out the dough with a rolling pin to about ¼–½ inch thick and cut out the crackers with a knife or cookie cutter.
3. Line a baking sheet with parchment paper and place the crackers on it.
4. Bake at 380°F for 15–20 minutes.

Dried Fruit Cookies

Prep time: 10 minutes

- Cooking time: 15 minutes
- Servings: 10

Nutritional Values:

- Calories 340
- Total carbs 33 g
- Protein 6.4 g
- Total fat 20.3 g

Ingredients:

- 2 cups oat flakes, toasted with butter in a frying pan
- 1 stick butter (4 oz)
- 1 egg
- 1 cup milk
- 2 tbsp coconut chips
- 2 0z almonds, ground
- 2 oz hazelnuts, ground
- 1¾ 0z prunes, chopped
- 1 tsp cinnamon
- 4 tbsp erythritol

Directions:

1. Combine oats, nuts, prunes, cinnamon and erythritol
2. Add milk and coconut, mix well.
3. Add the egg and give a good stir.
4. Shape the batter into cookies. Line a baking sheet with parchment paper and place the cookies on it.
5. Bake at 390°F for 15 minutes.

Ginger Cookies

Prep time: 10 minutes

- Cooking time: 15 minutes
- Servings: 10

Nutritional Values:

- Calories 21
- Total carbs 2.4 g
- Protein 1.6 g
- Total fat 1.1 g

Ingredients:

- 3 tbsp oat bran
- 2 egg whites
- 1 tbsp dried ginger
- 1 tsp plain cow's milk yogurt
- 1 tsp baking powder
- Sweetener of your choice to taste

Directions:

1. Combine all ingredients. Add more bran if the dough is too runny. Mix well.
2. Line a baking sheet with parchment paper and spoon the cookies onto it
3. Bake at 356°F for 15 minutes.

Chocolate Chip Cookies

Prep time: 10 minutes

- Cooking time: 15 minutes
- Servings: 15

Nutritional Values:

- Calories 195
- Total carbs 5 g
- Protein 4 g
- Total fat 16 g

Ingredients:

- 1 cup coconut flour
- ½ cup butter, soft
- 1 cup unsweetened coconut flakes
- 4 eggs
- 2 2/3 oz dark chocolate chips
- ½ tsp vanilla extract
- ½ cup erythritol

Directions:

1. Mix the salt, eggs, vanilla, erythritol and butter together.
2. Add the coconut flakes, coconut flour and chocolate chips. Stir and mix well. Line a baking sheet with parchment paper and spoon the cookies onto it.
3. Bake at 375°F for 15–20 minutes.

Eggplant Mufffins

Prep time: 15 minutes

- Cooking time: 20 minutes
- Servings: 3

Nutritional Values:

- Calories 194
- Total carbs 5.7 g
- Protein 8 g
- Total fat 14.2 g

Ingredients:

- 2 eggplants, peeled and cubed
- ¾ cup mozzarella
- 2 tbsp butter, melted
- 1 tbsp fresh basil, chopped
- 1 tsp garlic powder
- ½ tsp dried basil

Directions:

1. Preheat the oven to 374°F.
2. Mix garlic powder and dried basil, and add melted butter.
3. Place the cubed eggplant on the bottom of 3 baking cups.
4. Sprinkle with mozzarella and 1 tsp melted butter mixture.
5. Layer the eggplants again, then cheese, then butter.
6. Sprinkle with the remaining cheese.
7. Bake for 20 minutes until golden.

Japanese Cookies

- Servings: 8 cookies

Prep time: 10 minutes

Nutritional Values:

- Calories 46
- Total carbs 10 g
- Protein 3.6 g
- Total fat 1.6 g

Ingredients:

- 1 egg yolk
- Cooking time: 10 minutes
- 2 tbsp powdered milk + 1 tsp cow's milk
- 1 tbsp cocoa powder
- 2 tbsp erythritol
- 1 tbsp starch

Directions:

1. Whisk egg yolk with erythritol until well combined.
2. Add starch, powdered milk, cocoa powder and milk. Knead the dough and shape it into a ball.
3. With your hands roll the ball out to form a long " snake" Cut it and form small balls
4. Line a baking sheet with parchment paper .Form the small balls into cookies and place them on the paper.
5. Bake at 320° F for 10 minutes.
6. Use chopped peanuts instead of cocoa powder for white Japanese cookies.

Protein Buns

Prep time: 10 minutes

- Cooking time: 40 minutes
- Servings: 8

Nutritional Values:

- Calories 29
- Total carbs 0.1 g
- Protein 6.4g
- Total fat 0.3 g

Ingredients:

- 2 eggs
- ½ cup water
- 1½–2 oz soya protein powder
- Stevia to taste (1 dash)
- Cinnamon or vanilla
- extract to taste

Directions:

1. Whisk eggs, and then add other ingredients and whisk well.
2. Divide between 8 greased silicone cups and bake at 430°F for 20 minutes.
3. Lower the temperature to 340°F and bake for 10–15 minutes more.

Chapter 2: Lunch Recipes

Pumpkin Muffins

almonds - .25 cup

Servings: 5

Nutritional Values:

3.5 g Net Carbs;

7.4 g Proteins;

13.5 g Fat; 185 Calories

Ingredients:

- Salt - .5 tsp.
- Baking powder - .5 tsp.
- Egg – 1
- Vanilla extract – 1 tbsp.
- Apple cider vinegar – 1 tbsp.
- Pumpkin puree - .5 cup
- Coconut oil – 2 tbsp.
- Sugar-free caramel syrup - .25 cup
- Optional: Crushed

Directions:

1. Warm up the oven to 350°F. Combine all of the components in the recipe list except for the almonds.
2. Prepare a muffin pan for 5 portions. If you are using the almonds, spritz with some of the oil. Bake for 15-18 minutes. Enjoy for breakfast or on-the-go.

Pumpkin Maple Flaxseed Muffins

Servings: 10 **Nutritional Values:**

2 g Net Carbs; 5 g Proteins;

8.5 g Fat; 120 Calories

Ingredients:

- Ground flaxseeds – 1.25 cups
- Baking powder - .5 tbsp.
- Erythritol - .33 cup
- Salt - .5 tsp.
- Cinnamon – 1 tbsp.
- Pumpkin pie spice – 1 tbsp.
- Coconut oil – 2 tbsp.
- Pure pumpkin puree – 1 cup
- Egg - 1
- Maple syrup - .5 cup
- Apple cider vinegar - .5 tsp.
- Vanilla extract - .5 tsp.
- Topping: Pumpkin seeds

Also Needed:

- Blender such as NutriBullet
- Muffin tin – 10 sections with silicone liners

Directions:

1. Heat the oven to 350°F. Prepare the muffin tin with cupcake liners.
2. Toss the seeds into the blender about 1 second – no longer or it could become damp.
3. Combine the dry fixings and whisk until well mixed. Add the puree, vanilla extract, and pumpkin spice along with the maple syrup (.5 tsp.) if using. Blend in the oil, egg, and apple cider vinegar. Combine nuts or any other fold-ins of your choice, but also add the carbs.
4. Scoop the mixture out by the tablespoon into the prepared tins. Garnish with some of the pumpkin seeds. Leave a little space in the top since they will rise.
5. Bake approximately 20 minutes. They are ready when they are slightly browned. Let them cool a few minutes and add some ghee or butter or some more syrup.

Fathead Rolls

Servings: 4 – 2 per serving

Nutritional Values:

2.5 g Net

Carbs ; 7 g

Proteins;

13 g Fat;

160 Calories

Ingredients:

- Shredded mozzarella cheese - .75 cup
- Cream cheese – 2 oz. - 4 tbsp.
- Shredded cheddar cheese - .5 cup
- Beaten egg – 1
- Garlic powder - .25 tsp.
- Almond flour - .33 cup
- Baking powder – 2 tsp.

Directions:

1. Heat up the oven to 425°F.
2. Combine the mozzarella and cream cheese. Place in the microwave. Cook for about 20 seconds at a time until the cheese melts.
3. In another container, beat the egg and add the dry fixings.
4. Fold the plastic wrap over the dough. Gently start working into a ball. Be sure it is covered and place in the fridge for 1/2 hour.
5. Slice the dough ball into four sections and roll each one into a ball. Cut the ball in half (top and bottom of the bun).
6. Place the cut side down onto a well-greased sheet pan. Bake for 10 to 12 minutes. Fix them like you like them.

Squash Muffins

Servings: 6 **Nutritional Values:**

3.4 g Net Carbs;

7.3 g Proteins;

7.8 g Fat; 111 Calories

Ingredients:

- Salt – to taste
- Baking powder - .66 tsp.
- Almond flour – 1 cup
- Peeled & grated squash – 1
- Chopped spring onions – 2-3 sprigs
- Olive oil – 1 tbsp.
- Egg – 1
- Plain yogurt - .25 cup
- Grated hard cheese - .5 cup

Directions:

1. Warm up the oven to 350°F. Spritz six muffin tins with cooking oil spray.
2. Season the grated squash with salt and set aside.
3. Combine the baking powder, salt, and sifted flour.

4. Whisk the egg, and mix with the oil, 1/2 of the cheese, and yogurt. Combine the fixings.
5. Add the squash and juices to the dough. Work in the chopped onions and add to the prepared muffin cups (1/2 full). Sprinkle with the cheese and bake for 25 minutes.
6. Cool slightly and serve. Store in the fridge when cooled if you have leftovers.

Zucchini Bread – Slow- Cooked

Servings: 12 **Nutritional Values:**

13.8 g Net Carbs; 5 g Proteins;

15.7 g Fat; 174 Calories

Ingredients:

- Cinnamon - 2 tsp.
- Almond flour – 1 cup
- Coconut flour - .33 cup
- Optional: Xanthan gum - .5 tsp.
- Salt - .5 tsp.
- Baking soda - .5 tsp.
- Baking powder – 1.5 tsp.
- Softened coconut oil/butter - .33 cup
- Eggs - 3
- Vanilla – 2 tsp.
- Sweetener – 1 cup or Pyure all-purpose - .5 cup
- Shredded zucchini – 2 cups
- Chopped pecans/walnuts - .5 cup
- Also Needed: 8 x 4 silicone bread
    - pan

Directions:

1. Combine the coconut and almond flour, salt, baking soda and powder, xanthangum, and cinnamon. Set aside for now.
2. Mix the oil, eggs, vanilla, and sugar in another dish. Combine the fixings.
3. Blend in the nuts and shredded zucchini. Scoop the mixture into the prepared bread pan.
4. Arrange the cooker on the top rack (or on crunched up aluminum foil balls). You want it at least 1/2-inch from the bottom of the slow cooker.
5. Secure the top tightly, and cook for three hours on the high setting.
6. Cool and wrap the bread in a sheet of foil. It's best when refrigerated.

Biscuits & Gravy

Servings: 8

Nutritional Values:

5 g Net Carbs;

17.4 g Proteins;

40 g Fat;

460 Calories

Ingredients for the Biscuits:

- Baking powder – 1 tsp.
- Almond flour – 1 cup
- Celtic sea salt - .25 tsp.
- Egg white - 4
- Organic butter/cold coconut oil – 2 tbsp.
- Optional: Garlic or another preferred spice – 1 tsp.

Ingredients for the Gravy:

- Chicken/beef broth – 1 cup
- Cream cheese – 1 cup
- Ground black pepper – 1 pinch
- Celtic sea salt – to your liking
- Organic crumbled pork sausage - 1 pkg. (10 oz.)
- Also Needed: Coconut oil cooking spray

Directions:

1. Program the oven setting to 400°F. Prepare a muffin pan/cookie sheet with the cooking spray.
2. Cut the butter up into pieces – making sure they are cold. Whisk the whites until fluffy.
3. In another container, combine the flour and baking powder. Cut in the butter and add the salt. Fold in the mixture over the egg whites.
4. Drop the dough onto the baking pan/muffin tin. Bake 11-15 minutes.

Buttery Garlic & Sharp Cheddar Biscuits

144 Calories

Servings: 8 Nutritional Values:

0.5 g Net Carbs;

6.7 g Proteins;

12.8 g Fat;

Ingredients:

- Eggs - 4
- Melted – slightly cooled – butter - .25 cup
- Baking powder - .25 tsp.
- Sifted coconut flour - .33 cup
- Salt - .25 tsp.
- Garlic powder - .25 tsp.
- Shredded sharp cheddar cheese - 1 cup

Directions:

1. Set the oven temperature to 400°F. Cover a baking tin with a sheet of aluminum foil. Grease with a spritz of oil.
2. Whisk the garlic powder, butter, eggs, and salt together. Fold in the baking powder and flour. Whisk until the lumps are removed. Stir in the cheese, mixing well.
3. Drop by the ice cream scoopful onto the baking pan. Bake about 15 min. Leave it in the pan to cool for 5 to 10 minutes. Remove and serve.
4. They will lose the crispy texture if you don't cool first before you add them to a

storage container.

Cheddar Bay Biscuits

Servings: 4 - 8 biscuits – 2 per

serving Nutritional Values:

2 g Net

Carbs ;

20 g Fat;

13 g Protein;

230 Calories

Ingredients:

Shredded mozzarella cheese – 1.5 cups

- Shredded cheddar cheese – 1 cup
- Cream cheese – .5 of 1 pkg. - 4 oz.
- Large eggs – 2
- Almond flour - .66 cup
- Granulated garlic powder - .5 tsp.
- Baking powder - 4 tsp.
- Butter – for the pan

Directions:

1. Microwave the cream cheese and mozzarella for about 45 seconds using the high-power setting until melted. Stir and return for 20 additional seconds. Stir once more.
2. In another container, combine the eggs with the almond flour, garlic powder, and baking powder. Mix it all together and place on a sheet of flour-dusted plastic wrap. Roll it up into a ball and place in the fridge for 20-30 minutes.
3. Heat up the oven to reach 425ºF. Prepare a dark color baking dish with butter. Slice the cold dough into eight segments. Place in the prepared pan – leaving a little space between each one.
4. Bake for 10-12 minutes. Remove and place on the countertop to cool.

Lavender Biscuits

Servings: 6

270 Calories

Nutritional Values:

4 g Net Carbs;

10 g Proteins;

25 g Fat;

Ingredients:

- Coconut oil - .33 cup
- Baking powder – 1 tsp.
- Almond flour – 1.5 cups
- Kosher salt – 1 pinch
- Egg whites - 4
- Culinary grade lavender buds – 1 tbsp.
- Liquid stevia – 4 drops

Directions:

1. Warm up the oven until it reaches 350ºF. Spritz a baking sheet with a little coconut oil. Mix the coconut oil and almond flour in a container until it's in pea-sized pieces. (It's easier to use your hands.) Set the bowl aside in the fridge.
2. Whisk the eggs until they start foaming. Toss in the salt, lavender, and baking powder. Stir well and mix in the eggs. Add to the almond mixture, stirring well.
3. Place the chunks onto the baking sheet using an ice cream scoop or tablespoon. Pat them, so they aren't round similar to a pancake.
4. Bake for 20 minutes and enjoy.

Chapter 3 : Dinner

Macadamia Bread

Ingredients:

- Macadamia nuts – 2 cups
- Eggs - 4
- Almond flour - .25 cup
- Ground flax seed – 2 tbsp.
- Softened ghee - .25 cup
- Softened coconut butter - .5 cup
- Sea salt – 1 tsp.
- Baking powder - .5 tsp.
- Apple cider vinegar - 2 tbsp.
- Also Needed: 8 x 4 loaf pan

Servings: 16 **Nutritional Values:** 227 Cal.
5 g Net Carbs ;

5 g Prot. ;

22 g Fat ;

Directions:

1. Warm up the oven to 350°F. Lightly grease the pan with ghee.
2. Process the nuts using the S-blade in the food processor until they are a fine flour. Add the eggs - 1 at a time – with the motor running until the mixture is creamy.
3. Fold in the flaxseed, almond flour, coconut butter, ghee, vinegar, sea salt, and baking powder. Continue processing until well combined and pour into the prepared pan.
4. Bake for 35 to 40 minutes.
5. Cool the bread before slicing to serve or store.

Kale Crackers

Servings:20

Nutritional Values: Calories: 88,

Total Fat: 10.2 g,

Saturated Fat: 1.5 g, Carbs: 5.4 g,

Sugars: 0.4 g,

Protein: 4.6 g

Ingredients:

- 2 cup Almonds, soaked overnight, drained and rinsed, finely chopped
- 1 cup Coconut Flour
- 3/4 cup Nutritional Yeast
- 1 tsp Chipotle
- 1 tsp Smoked Paprika
- 1 cup Ground Flax Seeds, soaked in 1 cup water
- 1 bunch Kale, chopped
- Himalayan Salt, to taste
- Black Pepper, to taste

Directions:

1. Line a baking sheet with parchment paper and set aside.
2. Combine the almonds, coconut flour, nutritional yeast, chipotle, and paprika. Addthe kale and mix well.
3. Pour in the flax and water mixture, season with salt and pepper, and knead the dough.
4. Transfer the dough to a sheet of parchment paper, cover with another sheet and roll out the dough. Cut into crackers, place them on the prepared sheet and dehydrate at 290F / 145C for half an hour. Reduce the heat to 245F / 118C and dehydrate the crackers for about 8 hours, flipping halfway through.

. Chili Crackers

Servings:30 crackers

Nutritional Values:

Calories: 49,

Total Fat: 4.1 g, Saturated Fat: 1.2 g,

Carbs: 2.8 g,

Sugars: 0.1 g,

Protein: 1.6 g

Ingredients:

- ¾ cup Almond Flour
- ¼ cup Coconut Flour
- ¼ cup Flax Seed
- ½ tsp Paprika
- ½ tsp Cumin
- 1 1/2 tsp Chili Pepper Spice
- 1 tsp Onion Powder
- ½ tsp Salt
- 1 Egg¼ cup Unsalted Butter
-

Directions:

1. Preheat your oven to 350F / 175C. Line a baking sheet with parchment paper and set aside.
2. Add the ingredients to your food processor and pulse until dough forms.
3. Divide the dough into two equal parts. Place one ball on a sheet of parchment pepper, cover with another sheet and roll it out. Cut into crackers and repeat the same with the other ball of dough. Transfer the crackers to the prepared baking tray.
4. Bake for about 8-10 minutes. When done, remove from the oven, leave to cool and serve.

. Almond & Flax Crackers

Servings:20-24 crackers **Nutritional Values:** Calories: 47.7,

Total Fat: 5.2 g, Saturated Fat: 1 g, Carbs: 1.2 g,

Sugars: 0.1 g,

Protein: 1.9 g

Ingredients:

- ½ cup Ground Flax Seeds
- ½ cup Almond Flour
- 1 Tbsp Coconut Flour
- 2 Tbsp Shelled Hemp Seeds
- ¼ tsp Fine Sea Salt, plus more to sprinkle on top
- 1 Egg White
- 2 Tbsp Unsalted Butter, melted
-

Directions:

1. Preheat your oven to 300F / 150C. Line a baking sheet with parchment paper and set aside.
2. Combine the flax, almond, and coconut flour, hemp seed, and salt. Add the egg and melted butter and mix until well combined.
3. Transfer the dough onto a sheet of parchment paper, cover with another sheet of paper and roll out the dough. Cut into crackers and arrange them on the prepared baking sheet.
4. Bake for half an hour, allow to cool and serve.

Roasted Herb Crackers

Servings: 75 crackers

Protein: 1.3 g

Nutritional Values:

Calories: 34,

Total Fat: 5.1 g, Saturated Fat: 0.3 g, Carbs: 1.5 g,

Sugars: 0.3 g,

Ingredients:

- ¼ cup Avocado Oil
- 10 Celery Stalks
- 1 sprig Fresh Rosemary, stem discarded
- 2 sprigs Fresh Thyme, stems discarded
- 2 Tbsp Apple Cider Vinegar
- 1 tsp Himalayan Salt
- 3 cups Ground Flax Seed

Directions:

1. Preheat your oven to 225F / 110C. Line a baking sheet with parchment paper and set aside.
2. Add the oil, celery, herbs, vinegar, and salt to your food processor and pulse until pureed. Add the flax and pulse again to incorporate and let sit for about 2-3 minutes until the mixture firms up.
3. Transfer the batter to the prepared baking sheet, spread evenly and cut into crackers.

4. Bake in the preheated oven for about an hour. Remove the parchment paper, flip the crackers and bake for one more hour. If the crackers are thick, they will need more time to bake.
5. Once done, remove from the oven and leave t cool before serving.

No-Bake Coconut Bars

Preparation Time: 1 hour

Cooking Time:

Servings:5

Nutritional

Values:

- Fat: 13 g.
- Protein: 1 g.
- Carbs: 4 g.

Ingredients:

- 1 cup Shredded Coconut
- ½ cup Coconut Cream
- ½ cup Erythritol

Directions:

1. Combine all ingredients in a bowl. Mix until well combined.
2. Press the mixture into a rectangular silicon mold and freeze for an hour to set.
3. Slice for serving.

No-Bake Keto Mousse Cake

Preparation Time:

1 hour Nutrients

per serving:

- Cooking Time:
- Servings:8
- Nutritional Values:
- Fat: 38 g.
- Protein: 8 g.
- Carbs: 10 g.

Ingredients:

For the Crust

- 1.5 cups Almond Flour
- ¼ cup Unsweetened Cocoa Powder
- ¼ cup Erythritol
- ½ cup Melted Butter

For the Filling

- 1.5 cups Cream Cheese
- ½ cup Dark Chocolate Chips, melted
- ½ cup Erythritol
- 1 tsp Vanilla Extract
- 1 tbsp Gelatin
- 1 cup Boiling Water

Directions:

1. Combine all ingredients for the crust in a bowl. Mix well. Pack the mixture into a 9-inch springform pan.
2. Combine gelatin and erythritol in a bowl. Stir in a cup of boiling water. Leave for 5 minutes.
3. Beat cream cheese, melted chocolate, and vanilla in a separate bowl until light and airy.
4. Gradually stir in the gelatin mixture into the cream cheese mixture. Chill the mixture for 30 minutes then spread onto the crust.
5. Set the prepared cake in the chiller until ready to serve.

No-Bake Pumpkin Pie

Preparation Time: 8

hours Servings:8

Nutritional Values:

- Fat: 29 g.
- Protein: 7 g.
- Carbs: 9 g.
- Ingredients:

Ingredients:

For the Crust

- 1 cup Walnuts, chopped
- 1 cup Almond Flour
- ¼ cup Erythritol
- 1/3 cup Melted Butter

For the Filling

- 1 14-oz can Pumpkin Puree
- ½ cup Erythritol
- 1 cup Heavy Cream
- 6 Egg Yolks
- 1 tbsp Gelatin
- 1 tsp Vanilla Extract
- 1 tsp Cinnamon Powder
- ¼ tsp Ground Ginger
- ¼ tsp Ground Nutmeg

- ¼ tsp Ground Cloves

Directions:

1. Combine all ingredients for the crust in a bowl. Mix well. Pack the mixture into a 9-inch springform pan.
2. Combine all ingredients for the filling in a pot. Whisk over medium heat until mixture starts to thicken.
3. Pour filling into the crust and refrigerate overnight.

Crispy Almond Crackers

Servings:40 crackers

Nutritional Values:

Calories: 21.7,

Total Fat: 2.9 g,

Saturated Fat: 0.2 g,

Carbs: 0.8 g,

Sugars: 0.1 g,

Protein: 0.9 g

Ingredients:

- 1 cup Almond Flour
- 1/4 tsp Baking Soda
- 1/4 tsp Salt
- 1/8 tsp Black Pepper
- 3 Tbsp Sesame Seeds
- 1 Egg, beaten
- Salt and Black Pepper, to top the crackers

Directions:

1. Preheat your oven to 350F / 175C. Line two baking sheets with parchment paper and set aside.
2. Mix all the dry ingredients to a large bowl. Add the egg and mix well to incorporate and form a dough. Divide the dough into two balls.
3. Roll out the dough between two pieces of parchment paper. Cut into crackers and transfer them to the prepared baking sheet.
4. Bake for about 15-20 minutes. In the meantime, repeat the same procedure with the remaining dough.
5. Once done, leave the crackers to cool and serve.

No-Bake Tiramisu Cups

Preparation Time: 2 hours

Servings:8

Nutritional Values:

- Fat: 37 g.
- Protein: 5 g.
- Carbs: 5 g.
- Ingredients:

Ingredients:

For the Crust

- 1 cup Pecans, ground
- 1/3 cup Melted Butter
- 1 tbsp Unsweetened Cocoa Powder
- 2 tbsp Erythritol
- For the Filling
- 2 cups Mascarpone Cheese
- 1 shot Espresso
- ½ cup Erythritol
- 1 tsp Vanilla Extract
- 1 tbsp Gelatin
- 1 cup Boiling Water

Directions:

1. Combine all ingredients for the crust in a bowl. Mix well. Pack the mixture into a silicon cupcake mold.
2. Combine gelatin and erythritol in a bowl. Stir in a cup of boiling water. Leave for 5 minutes.
3. Beat mascarpone cheese, espresso, and vanilla in a separate bowl until light and airy.
4. Gradually stir in the gelatin mixture into the whipped mascarpone.
5. Chill the mixture for 30 minutes.
6. Divide the mixture onto the cupcake mold and chill for an hour.

No-Bake Choco-Chip Blondies

Preparation Time:

1 hour **Servings:12**

Nutritional Values:

- Fat: 14 g.
- Protein: 5 g.
- Carbs: 7 g.

Ingredients:

- 1 cup Almond Flour
- ¾ cup Erythritol
- ¾ cup Almond Butter
- 1 tbsp Vanilla extract
- ½ cup Sugar-Free Chocolate Chips

Directions:

1. Mix together almond butter, coconut flour, erythritol, and vanilla extract in a bowl until well combined.
2. Fold in the chocolate chips.
3. Press the mixture into a rectangular silicon mold and freeze for an hour to set.
4. Slice for serving.

No-Bake Banana Bread

Preparation Time:

1 hour Servings:8

Nutritional Values:

- Fat: 8 g.
- Protein: 2 g.
- Carbs: 9 g.

Ingredients:

- 2 Medium Bananas, mashed
- ½ cup Coconut Flour
- ¼ cup Almond Butter
- 2 tbsp Erythritol
- ¼ cup Chopped Walnuts

Directions:

Combine all ingredients in a bowl. Mix until well combined.

Press the mixture into cupcake molds and freeze for an hour to set.

Low-Carb Red Velvet Pancakes

Preparation Time: 5 minutes **Cooking Time: 10 minutes** **Servings:4**

Nutritional Values:

- Fat: 29 g.
- Protein: 13 g.
- Carbs: 5 g.

Ingredients:

- ½ cup Cream Cheese
- 4 Eggs
- 2 tbsp Butter, melted
- ½ cup Almond Flour
- 1 tbsp Unsweetened Cocoa Powder
- 2 tbsp Erythritol
- 1 tsp Vanilla Extract
- ½ tsp Red Food Coloring

Directions:

1. Mix all ingredients in a blender.
2. Preheat a skillet and coat with non-stick spray.
3. Ladle in the batter and cook for 1-2 minutes per side.

Chapter 4: Snacks

Zucchini Muffins

Nutritional Values:

Ingredients:

Calories: 59,

Total Fat: 4.1

g,

Saturated Fat: 2.4

g, Carbs: 7.4 g,

Sugars: 0.3 g,

Protein: 2.3 g

Serves: 12 muffins

- 6 Tbsp Coconut Flour
- 1 Tbsp Ground Flax Seeds
- ⅓ cup Erythritol
- 1 ½ tsp Baking Powder
- 1 tsp Cinnamon
- ¼ tsp Baking Soda
- 3 Eggs
- ½ cup Grated Zucchini

- ⅓ cup Grated Carrot
- ¼ cup Unsweetened Almond Milk
- 2 Tbsp Coconut Oil, melted
- ½ tsp Apple Cider Vinegar

Directions:

1. Preheat your oven to 350F / 175C. Grease your muffin tin or line it with paper muffin cups and set aside.
2. Mix together the coconut flour, flax, erythritol, baking powder, cinnamon, and baking soda and set aside.
3. In another bowl, whisk together the eggs, zucchini, carrot, almond milk, coconut oil, and apple cider vinegar. Add to the dry ingredients and mix well until well combined.
4. Pour the batter into the tin and bake for about half an hour.
5. Remove from the oven and leave to cool before serving.

Cinnamon Muffin Swirls

Ingredients:

- 1 cup Cauliflower, cooked and cooled
- ¾ cup Keto-Friendly Protein Powder
- ½ cup Ground Peanuts
- 3 Eggs
- 1 Tbsp Coconut Oil
- 4 tsp Stevia
- 1 tsp Baking Powder
- 2 Tbsp Ghee, melted
- 1 Tbsp Cinnamon

Nutritional Values:

Calories: 424,

Total Fat: 27.5

g,

Saturated Fat: 7.4 g,

Carbs: 13.3 g,

Sugars: 6.6 g,

Protein: 36.3 g

Serves: 6

Directions:

1. Preheat your oven to 350F / 175C. Grease your muffin tin or line with paper muffin cups and set side.
2. Add the cauliflower, peanut butter powder, coconut oil, eggs, baking powder, and stevia and set aside.
3. Pour the batter into the muffin tin.
4. Combine the cinnamon and ghee and pour ½ teaspoon on top of each muffin. Use a toothpick to make swirls and bake for about 10 minutes.
5. Remove from the oven and leave to cool before serving.

. Pecan & Cranberry Muffins

Serves: 12 muffins

Nutritional Values:

Calories: 191.9,

Total Fat: 16.4 g,

Saturated Fat: 3.2 g,

Carbs: 12.4 g,

Sugars: 1.3 g,

Protein: 6 g

Ingredients:

- 2 Eggs
- 2 Tbsp Coconut Oil, melted
- ½ cup Orange Juice
- ½ Tbsp Orange Zest
- ¼ cup Erythritol
- ½ tsp Baking Soda
- ⅓ cup Coconut Flour
- 2⅓ cups Almond Flour
- ½ cup Chopped Pecans
- 1 cup Fresh Cranberries

Directions:

1. Preheat your oven to 350F / 175C. Line your muffin tin with paper muffin cups and set aside.
2. Beat the eggs, coconut oil, orange juice and zest, and erythrol. Add the baking soda and flours and mix well using an electric mixer.
3. Gently fold in the pecans and cranberries and fill the prepared tin with the batter.
4. Bake for about 25 minutes. When done, remove from the oven and allow to cool before serving.

. Keto Blueberry Muffins

Serves: 2

Ingredients:

- 3 Eggs
- 1/3 cup Erythritol Crystals
- 1/4 cup Coconut Milk
- 5 Tbsp Coconut Flour
- 1/2 cup Frozen Blueberries

Nutritional Values:

Calories: 176.8,

Total Fat: 7.5 g, Saturated Fat: 2.2 g,

Carbs: 18.5 g,

Sugars: 4.2 g,

Protein: 9.1 g

Directions:

1. Preheat your oven to 350F / 175C. Line your muffin tin with paper muffin cups and set aside.
2. Combine the eggs, erythritol, and coconut milk. Once well combined, add the coconut flour and mix well and leave the batter to rest for 5 minutes.
3. Gently fold in the blueberries and pour the batter into the prepared muffin tin.
4. Bake for about half an hour. Once done, remove and allow to cool before serving.

. Herb Buns

Nutritional Values:

Calories: 152.9,

Total Fat: 10.8 g,

Saturated Fat: 5.6

g, Carbs: 9.9 g,

Sugars: 0.1 g,

Protein: 4.2 g

Serves: 6

Ingredients:

- 4 Eggs
- 1/4 cup Arrowroot Flour
- 1/3 cup Coconut Flour
- 1 tsp Baking Powder
- 1/4 tsp Onion Powder
- 1/4 tsp Garlic Powder
- 1/4 tsp Dried Oregano
- 1/4 tsp Dried Parsley
- 1/4 tsp Dried Basil
- 1/4 tsp Salt

- 1/4 cup Butter, melted

Directions:

1. Preheat your oven to 350F / 175C. Line a baking sheet with parchment paper and set aside.
2. Whisk the eggs and add the arrowroot, coconut flour, and baking powder and mix well. Add the seasonings and butter and give the batter a good stir.
3. Use a 1/3 cup as a measure to make 6 mounds, arranging them on the prepared sheet.
4. Bake in the preheated oven for about 15 minutes.
5. Remove from the oven, allow to cool slightly and serve.

. Ultimate Keto Buns

Serves: 10 buns

Nutritional

Values: Calories:

192.7,

Total Fat: 13.1 g, Saturated

Fat: 1.2 g, Carbs: 12.4 g,

Sugars: 0.7 g,

Protein: 8.5 g

Dry ingredients:

- ½ cup Ground Flax Seeds
- 1 tsp Salt
- 1 tsp Baking Soda
- 2 tsp Onion Powder
- 2 tsp Garlic Powder
- 1 ½ cup Almond Flour
- 2 tsp Apple Cider Vinegar
- 5 Tbsp Sesame Seeds
- ⅔ cup Psyllium Husks
- ½ cup Coconut Flour

Wet ingredients:

- 2 cups Boiling Water
- 2 Eggs
- 6 Egg Whites

Directions:

1. Preheat your oven to 350F / 175C. Line a baking tray with parchment paper and set aside.
2. Combine the dry ingredients and add the egg whites, whole eggs and water.
3. Use a spoon to make buns and arrange them on the prepared tray. Sprinkle with sesame seeds and press lightly into the dough.
4. Bake in the preheated oven for about 50 minutes.
5. When done, allow the buns to cool, use immediately or store at room temperature.

. Sesame Keto Buns

Serves: 12 buns

Ingredients:

Nutritional Values:

Calories: 113,

Total Fat: 14.6 g,

Saturated Fat: 0.5 g,

Carbs: 10.6 g,

Sugars: 0.2 g,

Protein: 5 g

- 1 cup Coconut Flour
- 1 tsp Baking Powder
- 1 tsp Salt
- ½ cup Pumpkin Seeds
- ½ cup Sesame Seeds + ½ cup to coat the buns
- ½ cup Psyllium Powder
- 8 Egg Whites
- 1 cup Boiling Water

Directions:

1. Preheat your oven to 350F / 175C. Line a cookie sheet with parchment paper and set aside.
2. Mix together the dry ingredients and set aside.

3. Add the eggs to your blender, blend until foamy and add to the dry mixture. Mix well to incorporate.
4. Gradually pour in the water and stir to form dough. Use the dough to form buns.
5. Add the remaining ½ cup sesame seeds to a plate, place a bun on the plate and press gently to make the sesame seeds stick to it. Repeat with the remaining buns and arrange them on the prepared cookie sheet.
6. Bake in the preheated oven for about 50 minutes.
7. When done, remove from the oven, let it cool, use immediately or store at room temperature.

. Keto “Cheeseburger” Muffins

Serves: 9

Nutritional Values:

Calories: 212.3,

Total Fat: 16.2 g, Saturated Fat: 5 g,

Carbs: 3.9 g,

Sugars: 0.8 g,

Protein: 12.4 g

Ingredients:

For the hamburger filling:

- 16 oz Ground Beef
- 1/2 tsp Onion Powder
- 2 Tbsp Tomato Paste
- Salt, to taste
- 1/2 tsp Garlic Powder

Pepper, to taste

For the cheeseburger muffin buns:

- 1/2 cup Ground Flax Seeds
- 1/2 cup Almond Flour1 tsp Baking Powder
- 1/2 tsp Salt
- 1/4 tsp Pepper
- 1/4 cup Coconut Milk
- 2 Eggs
-

-

Directions:

To prepare the filling:

1. Heat a skillet on medium-high, add a dash of oil and the ground beef. Stir-fry for 2 minutes, add the remaining ingredients and cook until browned. Set aside.
2. Preheat your oven to 350F / 175C. Prepare your muffin tin or silicone muffin cups and set aside.
3. Combine the dry ingredients and set aside.
4. Whisk together the eggs and milk and gradually add them to the dry mix, stirring to incorporate.
5. Divide the batter into muffin cups or your muffin tin. Make dents in the middle of each to make space for the ground beef. Spoon the ground beef filling into each muffin cup.
6. Bake in the preheated oven for about 15-20 minutes.
7. One baked, remove from the oven, leave to cool for 10 minutes and serve.

Puffy Buns

Serves: 6 buns

Nutritional Values:

Calories: 195.5,

Total Fat: 17.9 g, Saturated Fat: 5 g, Carbs: 3 g, Sugars: 0.5 g, Protein: 6.7 g

Ingredients:

- 4 Eggs
- 4 Tbsp Lard, melted
- ½ cup Almond Flour
- 1/2 tsp Himalayan Salt
- 1 tsp Onion Flakes
- 1 Tbsp Rosemary
- 1 Tbsp Black Sesame Seeds
- 1 Tbsp White Sesame Seeds

Directions:

1. Preheat your oven to 430F / 220C. Prepare your jumbo muffin molds and set aside.
2. Add the eggs and lard to your blender or food processor. Pulse until combined, add the remaining ingredients and process until a batter is formed.
3. Pour the batter into the prepared molds and bake in the preheated oven for about 25-30 minutes.
4. Remove from the oven, allow to cool slightly, use immediately or store at room temperature.

. Tahini Buns

Serves: 3 buns

Nutritional Values:

Calories: 172.3,

Total Fat: 14.9 g, Saturated Fat: 2.4 g, Carbs: 6.3 g,

Sugars: 0.1 g,

Protein: 6.4 g

Ingredients:

- 1 Egg
- 5 Tbsp Tahini Paste
- 1/2 tsp Baking Soda
- 1 tsp Lemon Juice
- 1 pinch Salt

Directions:

1. Preheat your oven to 350F / 175C. Line a baking sheet with parchment paper and set aside.
2. Combine the ingredients until blended into a smooth batter.
3. Scoop the batter onto the prepared sheet forming buns. Bake in the preheated oven for about 15-20 minutes.
4. Once done, remove from the oven, allow to cool, use immediately or store.

. Pumpkin Seed Buns

Serves: 10 buns

Nutritional Values:

Calories: 189.7,

Total Fat: 13.6 g, Saturated Fat: 1.4 g,

Carbs: 7.8 g,

Sugars: 0.8 g,

Protein: 9.2 g

Dry ingredients:

- ½ cup Coconut Flour
- 1 1/2 cups Almond Flour
- ½ cup Ground Flax Seeds
- 1 tsp Onion Powder
- 1 tsp Garlic Powder
- 1 tsp Baking Soda
- 2 tsp Cream of Tartar
- 5 Tbsp Sesame Seeds
- 1 tsp Salt

Wet ingredients:

- 2 Eggs
- 6 Egg Whites

- 1 cup Warm Water
- 1/3 cup Psyllium Husk Powder

Directions:

1. Preheat your oven to 350F / 175C. Line a baking tray with parchment paper and set aside.
2. Mix together the dry ingredients and set aside.
3. In another bowl, whisk together the eggs and add the water and psyllium husk. Mix well until smooth and gradually add to the dry ingredients. Knead the dough until nice and smooth.
4. Roll the dough into buns and arrange them on the prepared tray and bake for about 50 minutes.
5. Once baked, remove from the oven, allow to cool, use immediately or store.

. Healthy Bagels

Ingredients:

- 1 cup Coconut Flour
- 1 Tbsp Baking Powder
- ¼ cup Psyllium Husk
- ½ cup Hemp Hearts
- ½ cup Sesame Seeds
- ½ cup Pumpkin Seeds
- 1 tsp Celtic Salt
- 6 Egg Whites
- 1 cup Boiling Water

Serves: 6 small bagels **Nutritional Values:** Calories: 213.4,

Total Fat: 15.2 g, Saturated Fat: 2.5 g,

Carbs: 9.5 g,

Sugars: 0.6 g,

Protein: 11.1 g

Directions:

1. Preheat your oven to 350F / 175C. Line your cookie sheet with parchment paper and set aside.
2. Mix together the dry ingredients and set aside.

3. Whip the egg whites in a blender or food processor until foamy, add the dry ingredients and blend until incorporated.
4. Pour in the boiling water and mix until a smooth dough forms.
5. Form 6 balls from the dough and make a hole into each ball with your thumb. Place the balls onto the prepared sheet, pressing them down gently to form bagels.
6. Sprinkle with poppy or sesame seeds and bake for about 55-60 minutes.
7. Remove from the oven when done, allow to cool, use immediately or store.

. Coconutty Bagels

Serves: 8 bagels

Ingredients:

- 4 Eggs, whites and yolks separated
- 1 cup Almond Butter, warmed
- 1 tsp Baking Soda
- 1 tsp Salt
- ¼ cup Lukewarm Water
- ¼ cup Coconut Milk
- 2 tsp Apple Cider Vinegar
- ¼ cup Coconut Flour, sifted

Nutritional Values:

Calories: 336.5,

Total Fat: 27.3 g, Saturated Fat: 3.1

g, Carbs: 144 g,

Sugars: 2.2 g,

Protein: 115 g

Directions:

1. Preheat your oven to 400F / 200C. Grease your bagel pan and set aside.
2. Add the egg yolks to the almond butter along with the baking soda. Season with salt, stir and add to the lukewarm water and coconut milk. Use an electric mixer to combine into a smooth paste.
3. In a separate bowl, beat the egg whites, gradually adding the apple cider vinegar. Set aside when the soft peaks form.
4. Mix in the coconut flour into the paste and add the egg whites. Mix again until incorporated.
5. Pour the batter into your bagel pan and bake for 5 minutes. Reduce the temperature to 300F / 150C and bake for 20 more minutes.
6. Remove from the oven, allow to cool, pop out and use immediately or store.

. Garlic Bagels

Serves: 6 bagels

Nutritional Values:

Calories: 193.4,

Total Fat: 15 g, Saturated Fat: 7.3

g, Carbs: 7 g,

Sugars: 0.2 g,

Protein: 7.7 g

Ingredients:

- 6 Eggs
- 1 1/2 tsp Garlic Powder
- 1/3 cup Butter, melted
- 1/2 tsp Salt
- 1/2 cup Coconut Flour, sifted
- 1/2 tsp Baking Powder

Directions:

1. Preheat your oven to 400F / 200C. Grease your bagel pan and set aside.
2. Whisk together the eggs, garlic powder, butter, and salt and set aside.
3. Mix together the coconut flour and baking powder and add to the egg mixture. Mix well until incorporated and a batter is formed with no lumps.
4. Pour the batter into the prepared bagel pan and bake for about 15 minutes.
5. Remove from the oven and allow to cool when done. Use immediately or store.

. Cauliflower Bagels

Serves: 12 bagels

Nutritional Values:

Calories: 53.1,

Total Fat: 5.8 g, Saturated Fat: 2.3 g, Carbs: 1.5 g,

Sugars: 0 g, Protein: 2 g

Ingredients:

- 1 large Cauliflower, divided into florets and roughly chopped
- ¼ cup Nutritional Yeast
- ¼ cup Almond Flour
- ½ tsp Garlic Powder
- 1 ½ tsp Fine Sea Salt
- 2 Eggs
- 1 Tbsp Sesame Seeds

Directions:

1. Preheat your oven to 400F / 200C. Line a baking sheet with parchment paper and set aside.
2. Blend the cauliflower in a food processor and transfer to a bowl. Add the nutritional yeast, almond flour, garlic powder, and salt and mix to combine.
3. In a separate bowl, whisk the eggs and add them to the cauliflower mixture. Give the dough a good stir to incorporate the eggs into the mixture.
4. Make balls from the dough, making a hole with your thumb into each ball. Arrange them on the prepared sheet, flattening them slightly to make the bagel shape.
5. Sprinkle with the sesame seeds and bake for about half an hour.
6. Remove from the oven, allow to cool, use immediately or store.

. Tender Crackers

Serves: 22 crackers

Ingredients:

- 1 cup Almond Flour
- 1 Tbsp Chopped Fresh Rosemary
- 1/4 tsp Salt
- 1/2 tsp Garlic Powder
- Dash of Pepper
- 2 Tbsp Melted Butter
- 2 Eggs
- 2 Tbsp Water

Nutritional Values:

Calories: 44.9,

Total Fat: 4 g, Saturated Fat: 1 g,

Carbs: 1.1 g,

Sugars: 0.2 g, Protein: 1.7 g

Directions:

1. Using a½ tbsp measure, drop the batter onto the prepared cookie sheet forming crackers.
2. Bake for about 5-8 minutes. Once baked and crispy, remove from the oven and serve.

•

Pesto Crackers

Serves: 6

Nutritional Values: Calories: 210.9, Total Fat: 19.8 g, Saturated Fat: 4.6 g, Carbs: 6 g, Sugars: 1 g, Protein: 6.1 g

Ingredients:

- 1 1/4 cups Almond Flour
- 1/2 tsp Baking Powder
- 1/2 tsp Salt
- 1/4 tsp Ground Black Pepper
- 1 Pinch Cayenne Pepper
- 1/4 tsp Dried Basil
- 1 Garlic Clove, pressed
- 2 Tbsp Basil Pesto
- 3 Tbsp Butter

Directions:

1. Preheat your oven to 325F / 160C. Line your cookie sheet with parchment paper and set aside,
2. Mix together the almond flour, baking powder, salt, and pepper. Stir in the cayenne, basil, and garlic. Once combined, add the pesto and mix until coarse crumbs are formed.
3. Add the butter and knead until a smooth dough forms.
4. Transfer the dough to the prepared sheet and spread it into a thin layer. Bake for about 15-20 minutes. When done, remove from the oven, allow to cool slightly and cut into crackers.

. Seed Crackers

Serves: 72 crackers

Ingredients:

- 1 cup Boiling Water
- 1/3 cup Chia Seeds
- 1/3 cup Sesame Seeds
- 1/3 cup Pumpkin Seeds
- 1/3 cup Flax Seed
- 1/3 cup Sunflower Seeds
- 1 Tbsp Psyllium Powder
- 1 cup Almond Flour
- 1 tsp Salt
- 1/4 cup Coconut Oil, melted

Nutritional Values:

Calories: 33.6,

Total Fat: 2.8 g,

Saturated Fat: 0.8

g, Carbs: 1.6 g,

Sugars: 0.1 g,

Protein: 1.1 g

Directions:

1. Preheat your oven to 300F / 150C. Line a cookie sheet with parchment paper and set aside.
2. Add all the ingredients except the coconut oil and water to your food processorand pulse until all the ingredients are ground. Transfer to a large mixing bowl.
3. Pour in the melted coconut oil and boiling water and mix until well combined.
4. Transfer to the prepared sheet and spread into a thin layer.
5. Cut the dough into crackers and bake for an hour. When done, allow the crackers to cool. Serve immediately or store in an airtight container.

. Salt & Pepper Crackers

Serves: 20 crackers

Nutritional Values:

Calories: 67.6,

Total Fat: 5.8 g,

Saturated Fat: 0.5

g, Carbs: 1.4 g,

Sugars: 0.4 g,

Protein: 2.7 g

Ingredients:

- 1 Egg
- 2 cups Almond Flour
- ½ tsp Celtic Sea Salt, plus more for sprinkling
- ½ tsp Ground Black Pepper, plus more for sprinkling

Directions:

1. Preheat your oven to 350F / 175C. Line a baking sheet with parchment paper and set aside.
2. Add the ingredients to your food processor and pulse until dough forms.
3. Place the dough on a sheet of parchment paper, cover with another piece of paper and roll it out into a thin layer. Transfer to the baking sheet and cut into crackers.
4. Sprinkle with salt and pepper and bake for about 10-15 minutes.
5. When done, remove, allow to cool and

serve.

. Chili Crackers

Serves: 30 crackers

Nutritional Values: Calories: 49,

Total Fat: 4.1 g,

Saturated Fat: 1.2 g,

Carbs: 2.8 g,

Sugars: 0.1 g,

Protein: 1.6 g

Ingredients:

- ¾ cup Almond Flour
- ¼ cup Coconut Flour
- ¼ cup Flax Seed
- ½ tsp Paprika
- ½ tsp Cumin
- 1 1/2 tsp Chili Pepper Spice
- 1 tsp Onion Powder
- ½ tsp Salt
- 1 Egg
- ¼ cup Unsalted Butter

Directions:

1. Preheat your oven to 350F / 175C. Line a baking sheet with parchment paper and set aside.
2. Add the ingredients to your food processor and pulse until dough forms.
3. Divide the dough into two equal parts. Place one ball on a sheet of parchment pepper, cover with another sheet and roll it out. Cut into crackers and repeat the same with the other ball of dough. Transfer the crackers to the prepared baking tray.
4. Bake for about 8-10 minutes. When done, remove from the oven, leave to cool and serve.

. Savory Italian Crackers

Serves: 20-30 crackers

Nutritional Values: Calories: 63.5, Total Fat: 5.8 g, Saturated Fat: 0.6 g, Carbs: 1.8 g, Sugars: 0.3 g, Protein: 2.1 g

Ingredients:

- 1 1/2 cup Almond Flour
- 1/4 tsp Garlic Powder
- 1/2 tsp Onion Powder
- 1/2 tsp Thyme
- 1/4 tsp Basil
- 1/4 tsp Oregano
- 3/4 tsp Salt
- 1 Egg

- 2 Tbsp Olive Oil

Directions:

1. Preheat your oven to 350F / 175C. Line a baking tray with parchment paper and set aside.
2. Combine all the ingredients into a food processor until dough forms.
3. Form the dough into a log and slice into thin crackers. Arrange the crackers onto the prepared baking sheet and bake for about 10-15 minutes.
4. When done, allow to cool and serve.

Almond & Flax Crackers

Serves: 20-24 crackers

Nutritional Values:

Calories: 47.7,

Total Fat: 5.2 g, Saturated Fat: 1 g,

Carbs: 1.2 g,

Sugars: 0.1 g, Protein: 1.9 g

Ingredients:

- ½ cup Ground Flax Seeds
- ½ cup Almond Flour
- 1 Tbsp Coconut Flour
- 2 Tbsp Shelled Hemp Seeds
- ¼ tsp Fine Sea Salt, plus more to sprinkle on top
- 1 Egg White
- 2 Tbsp Unsalted Butter, melted

Directions:

1. Preheat your oven to 300F / 150C. Line a baking sheet with parchment paper and set aside.
2. Combine the flax, almond, and coconut flour, hemp seed, and salt. Add the egg and melted butter and mix until well combined.
3. Transfer the dough onto a sheet of parchment paper, cover with another sheet of paper and roll out the dough. Cut into crackers and arrange them on the prepared baking sheet.
4. Bake for half an hour, allow to cool and serve.

. Coconut & Cauliflower Bread

Serves: 4 **Nutritional Values:** Calories: 272.8, Total Fat:

20.9 g, Saturated Fat: 3.8 g, Carbs: 11.5 g,

Sugars: 0.3 g,

Protein: 10.7 g

Ingredients:

- 1 small head Cauliflower, cleaned and chopped into small florets
- 1/4 cup Extra Virgin Olive Oil
- 1/2 tsp Salt
- Black Pepper, to taste
- 3/4 cup Coconut Flour
- 1 tsp Garlic Powder
- 1/2 tsp Baking Soda
- 6 Eggs
- 1/4 cup Almond Milk

Directions:

1. Preheat your oven broiler. Line a baking sheet with parchment paper.
2. Place the cauliflower on the baking sheet, drizzle with the olive oil and season with salt and pepper. Bake in the oven until roasted and tender.
3. In the meantime, mix together the remaining ingredients and set aside.
4. When the cauliflower is roasted, remove it from the oven and add to the batter. Do not turn off the oven but reduce the temperature to 350F / 175C.
5. Grease a loaf pan and pour in the batter and bake for about half an hour.
6. Once baked and golden brown, remove from the oven, leave to cool, slice and eat.

. Salty Rosemary Crackers

Serves: 36 crackers

Ingredients:

Nutritional Values:

Calories: 35.2,

Total Fat: 5.2 g, Saturated Fat: 1.9 g,

Carbs: 1 g,

Sugars: 0.2 g, Protein: 1.2 g

- 1 1/2 cup Almond Flour
- 1/2 tsp Celtic Sea Salt
- 1 Egg, room temperature
- 2 Tbsp Coconut Oil
- 1/4 tsp Black Pepper
- 1 Tbsp Finely Chopped Rosemary

Directions:

1. Preheat your oven to 350F / 175C. Line a baking tray with parchment paper and set aside.
2. Mix together the almond flour and salt and set aside.
3. In another bowl, whisk together the egg, coconut oil, black pepper, and rosemary. Add the mixture to the almond flour mix and mix well until dough forms.
4. Transfer the dough to a piece of parchment paper, cover with another piece and roll it out into a thin layer. Cut into crackers, arrange them on the prepared sheet and bake for about 10-15 minutes.
5. Allow to cool when done and serve.

CPSIA information can be obtained
at www.ICGtesting.com
Printed in the USA
LVHW060027200121
676908LV00028B/827

9 781801 593403